Cora and the Unicorn

Chapter 5
Lesson 77: Murmur Diphthong *OR*
Lexile® Measure: 560L

ISBN 978-1-62382-035-0

Cora lived alone in a little stone dwelling deep in the middle of the Ordale Forest. Each day she woke up smiling. She loved the sound of animals moving about through the trees and grass.

When she went into the forest to collect twigs, Cora talked to all of her animal friends. Each morning, Cora cleaned her home and went for a walk. Then, she would settle down on her fluffy sofa and read a good story.

One day as Cora sat reading, she heard a strange sound outside. It was the very soft whine of a horse.

"That could not be the sound of a horse!" said Cora to herself. "Horses do not live in the Ordale Forest."

Cora looked out from her home. Standing by the archway was a beautiful white horse.

She looked closer. She could see a horn coming from the middle of its forehead. Could it be a unicorn? Cora rubbed her eyes. She had never seen a unicorn before! Quickly, she ran out to the horse. When she got closer, she could see it had a big thorn stuck in its neck.

"Please, can you help me?" asked the unicorn. "My name is Storm. The animals in the forest said you were kind and would help me."

"Oh, yes," replied Cora. She gently plucked the thorn from Storm's neck. She said, "Please come and let me feed you so you can get well."

Storm and Cora went to the barn behind her home. There, she fed Storm some grain, roasted acorns, and fresh water. Then, she brushed his soft coat until it gleamed. "You have been so kind to me," snorted Storm. "Put your hand on my magic horn, and make a wish. Your wish will be granted."

Cora placed her hand on the horn. She shut her eyes. She wished the unicorn would be her friend and would live with her forever.

Storm looked at Cora. He bent his head, and said, "I cannot live with you. But all you have to do is call my name, and I will come to you. We will be forever friends."

The End

Comprehension Questions

1. This story is mainly about
   a. the life of a unicorn.
   b. the animals in Ordale Forest.
   c. a girl who helps a magic unicorn.

2. How did Cora help Storm?
   a. She gave him a saddle.
   b. She took him back to his family.
   c. She took the thorn out of his neck.

3. Cora lived in a little stone dwelling. Which could be a *dwelling* for a bird?
   a. a nest
   b. a cave
   c. a doghouse

4. After reading this story, what do you know about Ordale Forest?

    a. It is not a safe place to live.

    b. There are many traffic lights.

    c. It is a peaceful place with many friendly animals.

5. What did Cora wish for?

    a. a bigger house

    b. someone to do her homework

    c. that the unicorn would be her friend forever

Skill Words

Cora	story	unicorn	snorted
Ordale	horse	thorn	forever
forest	horses	storm	
morning	horn	acorns	

Most Common Words

a	eyes	me	to
about	for	move	tree
all	friend	moving	trees
alone	friends	my	up
and	from	name	very
animal	get	not	walk
animals	good	of	was
as	had	on	water
asked	hand	one	we
at	have	out	well
be	he	placed	went
been	her	put	were
big	his	reading	when
but	home	said	will
by	I	see	with
call	in	she	would
can	into	so	you
come	is	some	your
coming	it	sound	
could	kind	that	
day	little	the	
do	live	then	
down	looked	there	
each	make	through	

Challenge Words

loved	heard	forehead	magic
talked	beautiful	oh	head